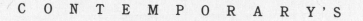
CONTEMPORARY'S

CHOICES
AN ESL LIFESKILLS SERIES FOR ADULTS
DISCOVERING YOUR COMMUNITY

CONTEMPORARY'S

CHOICES
AN ESL LIFESKILLS SERIES FOR ADULTS
DISCOVERING YOUR COMMUNITY

CAROLINE T. LINSE

Project Editor
Marietta Urban

Consultants
Ann Van Slyke
ESL Consultant
Atlanta, Georgia

Terence J. Bray
Hacienda La Puente
Unified School District
Hacienda Heights, California

CB
CONTEMPORARY
BOOKS
CHICAGO

Linse, Caroline T.
    Discovering your community / Caroline T. Linse.
        p.   cm. — (Choices : an ESL lifeskills series for adults)
    Includes index.
    ISBN 0-8092-4042-4 (pbk.)
      1. Readers for new literates.   2. Community life—Problems,
exercises, etc.   3. Readers—Community life.   I. Linse,
Caroline T.   II. Title.   III. Series: Choices (Chicago, Ill.)
PE1126.A4Y4   1991
428.6'2.—dc20   91-32022
                                          CIP

Choices: An ESL Lifeskills Series for Adults was developed
for Contemporary Books by **Quest Editorial Development,
Inc.** David Tillyer, Editor.

This book is dedicated to Harriet Leon with thanks for
providing learning opportunities.

Published by Contemporary Books, Inc.
180 North Michigan Avenue, Chicago, Illinois 60601
Manufactured in the United States of America
International Standard Book Number: 0-8092-4042-4

Published simultaneously in Canada by
Fitzhenry & Whiteside
195 Allstate Parkway
Valleywood Business Park
Markham, Ontario L3R 4T8
Canada

Editorial Director	*Editorial Production Manager*
Caren Van Slyke	Norma Fioretti
Senior Editor	*Production Editor*
Julie Landau	Marina Micari
Editorial	*Cover Design*
Chris Benton	Georgene Sainati
Lisa Black	
Lisa Dillman	*Illustrator*
Eunice Hoshizaki	Gary Undercuffler
Charlotte Ullman	
Cliff Wirt	*Typography*
	Terrence Alan Stone
Editorial Assistant	
Erica Pochis	Cover photograph © C. C. Cain

■■■■■ Contents

■ ■ ■ ■ ■ To the Student

Welcome to *Discovering Your Community*!

Discovering Your Community is part of Contemporary's **Choices: An ESL Lifeskills Series for Adults**.

The purpose of this book is to give you information about resources that can be found in your local area. **Discovering Your Community** will also give you the language skills you need to use that information.

You already know about community resources in your native country. **Discovering Your Community** encourages you to compare the way you do things in your native country with the way you do things in the United States.

Discovering Your Community offers valuable information about:

- adult education programs
- employment and unemployment
- community television
- library resources
- community recreation and athletics
- public transportation
- community mental health resources
- telephones and mail service
- emergency services

and many other community resources.

We hope you enjoy **Discovering Your Community**.

Level

Choices: An ESL Lifeskills Series for Adults is designed for ESL students who are at the intermediate level. **Choices** will guide students in making informed decisions about their lives in the U.S., based on the knowledge they bring from their native countries. **Choices** will help students acquire the life-skills competencies, language skills, and cultural information they need to make effective choices in the U.S.

Rationale

Discovering Your Community provides a student-centered approach to language learning. It offers detailed information about community resources in the U.S. while providing opportunities for cultural comparison and teaching practical language skills. The **Choices** series features natural language that adult students can put to immediate use in their daily lives.

Format

Discovering Your Community contains a *Tips for Teachers* section, twelve chapters, four review units, an appendix, and an index. The review units are interactive information-gap exercises that appear after every three chapters, incorporating content from those chapters. The authors acknowledge Judy Winn-Bell Olsen and Richard C. Yorkey as sources of inspiration for these exercises.

For step-by-step information on how to use this book and for additional classroom activities, see **Choices Teacher's Guide** 2.

Tips for Teachers

Everyone from the beginning teacher to the experienced professional can benefit from teaching suggestions. What follows are notes on the purpose of the sections in **Discovering Your Community** and how to use them.

The **Before You Listen** section prepares students for the dialogue by encouraging them to discuss the picture that illustrates it. Ask students to predict what they think will happen in the dialogue. This is a good time for you to assess how much the students know about the topic. If you want to emphasize key words before students listen to the dialogue, consult the. **Words to Know** section.

There are a number of ways to present the **Dialogue**. It is helpful to act out the dialogue, doing something to indicate that you are portraying different people talking. For example, you may want to use different voices or change positions as you change roles. If the resources are available, you may wish to record the dialogue ahead of time. If you do this, make sure each character is vocally distinct so that students know who is talking.

Discuss the dialogue, using the **Talking It Over** questions as a guide. Ask students if they have had experiences similar to the situation in the dialogue.

Assign different groups of students to different roles corresponding to the characters in the dialogue. Have them repeat their parts after you. Have students practice the dialogue in pairs or groups. Ask for volunteers to perform the dialogue for the class. Most of the dialogues are open-ended. Have students invent their own endings.

Words to Know presents vocabulary that students need to know to understand the dialogue. The blank lines allow students to personalize the text by adding their own words to the vocabulary list. Encourage students to guess the meaning of vocabulary from the context and to refer back to the picture.

Another Way to Say It offers alternatives for some of the idiomatic expressions that are introduced in the dialogue. Have students read the dialogue again, inserting the new expressions. The blank lines in this section allow students to personalize the text by adding their own expressions to the vocabulary list.

Talking It Over should foster discussion about the situation presented in the dialogue and invite students to talk about how their own experiences relate to the situation. The questions in this section range from simple comprehension to application of the information to students' lives.

In **Working Together**, a role-playing activity, students create conversations and put to use the language they have just learned. You may want to write the sample conversation on the board and ask students what they think should come next. Write their ideas on the board. After students have written the conversation as a class, have them practice it in pairs or groups, and ask for volunteers to role-play it for the class. Then have students create individual conversations based on relevant experiences.

Real Talk shows students how American English speakers really talk. For that reason, it's important not to overarticulate when you present this section.

Putting It Together presents grammar in context. It focuses on one useful structure that appears in the dialogue. There is a short presentation of the structure and then a contextualized exercise. This is followed by the opportunity to use the structure in meaningful, real-life responses.

In the **Read and Think** section, students are asked to guess the meanings of underlined words. The content reading on this page provides information that students can put to use immediately. The **Read and Think** page is not always a reading passage. It often consists of examples of the kinds of reading materials that people have to deal with every day, such as junk mail, fliers for community organizations, and paycheck stubs.

In Your Community offers students an opportunity to explore the community resources available to them. They can do this individually or in pairs or groups. You may also want to take students to a community-based organization during class time, invite a speaker to the classroom, or bring in realia such as a listing of local organizations and services.

Figuring Out the U.S. features an intimate look at one aspect of U.S. culture. Students are encouraged to circle any words in the passage that they don't understand and to try to guess their meanings from the context.

Your Turn gives the students the chance to compare life here with life in their native countries and opens up avenues to a variety of choices. Depending on the proficiency level of your students, the writing activity may range from a simple list to a paragraph expressing an opinion.

Are You Moving?

Before You Listen

1. Where are these people?
2. Why do you think they are there?
3. What do you think Mrs. Park and Mr. Cogam are talking about?
4. Who do you think the toys belong to?

■ ■ ■ ■ ■ Are You Moving?

Listen carefully to the dialogue.

Mrs. Park: Are you moving?

Mr. Cogam: Yes, we're moving in.

Mrs. Park: Welcome. My name is Irene Park. I live in apartment 27.

Mr. Cogam: It's nice to meet you. I'm Howard Cogam. My family is moving into apartment 32. Do you like it here?

Mrs. Park: I like it a lot now. I was pretty lonely at first. I used to live with my family in South Korea, and I moved here two years ago. Now I'm used to living in this community.

Mr. Cogam: We came to the U.S. five months ago. I miss my friends. My wife used to have a beautiful flower garden, and she misses that a lot. But we're all adjusting too.

Mrs. Park: Do you have children?

Mr. Cogam: Yes, we have three children, and my mother lives with us too.

Mrs. Park: Is it hard for your mother to get used to the U.S.?

Mr. Cogam: Oh, yes. She misses her friends a lot. I don't know what she'll do all day. My wife and I work, and our children will be in school . . .

Mrs. Park: Well, I made friends quickly when I started taking courses at the adult education center. Maybe she could do that too.

Words to Know

apartment	miss	all day
lonely	a lot	education
community	adjusting	_____

Another Way to Say It

moving in .... starting to live in a new place

pretty (lonely) .... very (lonely)

get used to .... adjust to, become accustomed to

_____ ...... _____

■ ■ ■ ■ ■ Talking It Over

Discuss the questions in pairs or groups.

1. Mrs. Park was very lonely at first. Is she happier now? Why or why not?
2. Why is Mr. Cogam worried about his mother?
3. What did you used to have in your native country that you miss?
4. What do you have now that you didn't use to have?
5. Is it easy or hard to make friends in the U.S.?
6. Is it easy for children and teenagers to move? Why or why not? What problems might they have?
7. Is it easy for older people to move? Why or why not? What problems might they have?
8. Why did you come to the U.S.? How did each person in your family feel about the decision?

Working Together

Before the Cogams moved, Mr. Cogam told his son Joe about their move. Joe is 16 years old. He was very upset about the move. He would be far away from his girlfriend, Violet. Work with your classmates and teacher to finish this conversation.

Joe:	I'm going to miss Violet.
Mr. Cogam:	I'm sorry, but we have to move.
Joe:	You don't understand. I love Violet!
Mr. Cogam:	
Joe:	

Real Talk

Listen to your teacher say this sentence:

Mrs. Cogam *used to* have a garden.

Used to sounds more like "use ta." Be sure to write *used to*.

Used to/Is Used to

Used to describes a situation that existed in the past, but does not exist now.

Mrs. Park **used to live** with her family in South Korea.

Is used to means "is accustomed to" something. It describes a situation that exists now.

Now Mrs. Park **is used to living** in the U.S.

(Note the *-ing* form of the verb after *is used to*.)

Practice A

Complete these sentences with *used to* or *is used to*.

1. Mrs. Park misses her grandmother. She ____*used to*____ visit her every week.

2. Mrs. Cogam _____ water her garden every day.

3. Now Mr. Cogam _____ living in the U.S.

4. Joe _____ seeing Violet every day.

5. Mrs. Park _____ live in South Korea.

6. Mrs. Park started taking classes at the adult education center last fall. Now she _____ taking classes at night.

Practice B

Work with a partner. Ask questions and give answers about what you used to do in your native country.

Example: Did you **use to** live with your family?*
Yes, I **used to** live with my parents.

Then talk about what you are/are not used to doing in the U.S.

Example: I'm **used to living** alone.
I'm **not used to eating** fast food.

*Note: Some people write this question as *Did you **used to** live with your family?* However, *Did you **use to**?* is the preferred written form.

■■■■■ Read and Think

Read the brochure and try to guess the meanings of the underlined words.
Rephrase each paragraph.

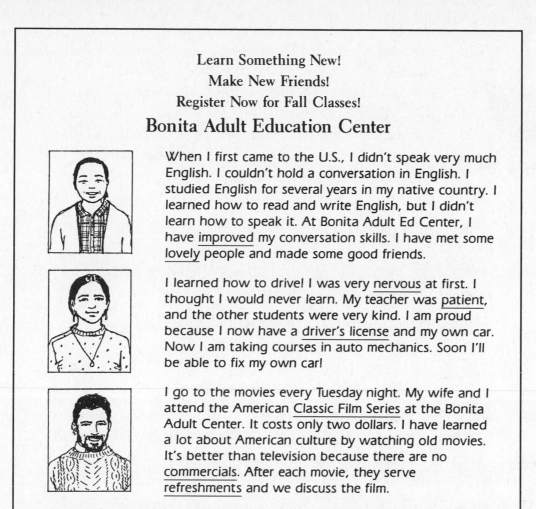

Learn Something New!
Make New Friends!
Register Now for Fall Classes!

Bonita Adult Education Center

When I first came to the U.S., I didn't speak very much English. I couldn't hold a conversation in English. I studied English for several years in my native country. I learned how to read and write English, but I didn't learn how to speak it. At Bonita Adult Ed Center, I have <u>improved</u> my conversation skills. I have met some <u>lovely</u> people and made some good friends.

I learned how to drive! I was very <u>nervous</u> at first. I thought I would never learn. My teacher was <u>patient</u>, and the other students were very kind. I am proud because I now have a <u>driver's license</u> and my own car. Now I am taking courses in auto mechanics. Soon I'll be able to fix my own car!

I go to the movies every Tuesday night. My wife and I attend the American <u>Classic Film Series</u> at the Bonita Adult Center. It costs only two dollars. I have learned a lot about American culture by watching old movies. It's better than television because there are no <u>commercials</u>. After each movie, they serve <u>refreshments</u> and we discuss the film.

In Your Community

Find out the information individually or in groups and share it with
the class.

1. Where do you take ESL classes? Are other courses offered there? Have you ever taken one?
2. What courses are offered at your local adult education center? community college? high school evening program?
3. Where can you go to meet people in your community?

■■■■■ Figuring Out the U.S.

As you read the passage, circle the words you don't understand and try to guess their meanings.

What Should I Call You?

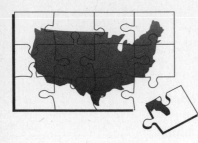

Knowing when to call someone by his or her first or last name is very difficult. This is confusing even for Americans who have lived in the United States all of their lives. Women may use the title *Miss, Mrs.,* or *Ms.* Some women keep their maiden names when they marry. Others change their family names to their husbands' family names. Here are some commonly asked questions about first and last names:

1. **I met someone at a party. He introduced himself as Jack Eng. What do I call him?**
   Jack. At parties, people usually call each other by their first names. Last names may be used if the party is formal or if older people are there.

2. **What is the difference between *Ms., Miss,* and *Mrs.*?**
   Ms. is used for all women, whether they are married or not. It is a modern term. *Miss* shows that a woman is unmarried. *Mrs.* shows that a woman is married. *Miss* and *Mrs.* are more traditional titles.

3. **If Tamara Colón marries Tom Wilkes, what will her married name be?**
   She has several choices. She could keep her maiden name and be Tamara Colón. She could take her husband's name and be Tamara Wilkes. She could also combine the two and become Tamara Colón-Wilkes.

4. **Do I call my boss by her first name or last name?**
   Many employers prefer to be called by their first names. But there are some who feel this is rude. If you are not sure, use his or her last name. Your employer may then say, "Call me by my first name."

Your Turn

Discuss the questions.

1. What do you call your employer? What did you call your employer in your native country?
2. When do people use family names in your native country?
3. Are people in the U.S. more or less formal than people in your native country?

> *Choose one of the questions and write about it.*

---

2 How Can They Do This to Me?

Before You Listen

1. Where are these people?
2. Why do you think they are there?
3. How do you think they feel?

■■■■■ How Can They Do This to Me?

Listen carefully to the dialogue.

Mrs. Park: I can't believe it! I'm being laid off!

Mr. Samuels: Oh no! I got a pink slip too.

Mrs. Park: How can Bonita Soups do this to me?

Mrs. Tamler: The last one hired is the first fired.

Mrs. Park: Does that mean they're going to keep Mr. Jenkins? He's the slowest guy here.

Mrs. Tamler: Yeah, they'll keep Jenkins. He's slow, but he has more seniority than any other employee.

Mr. Samuels: What do you mean he gets to stay? He doesn't do a thing!

Mrs. Park: It's not right! We work hard.

Mr. Samuels: We are the three fastest workers. The boss keeps telling us we're the best.

Mrs. Park: I just don't know what I'll do. How will I pay my rent?

Mrs. Tamler: I'm going to apply for unemployment compensation. I have to feed my kids. Then I'll start looking for a job.

Mr. Samuels: That may be OK for you. But I'm not going on welfare!

Mrs. Tamler: It's not welfare! Every week they take money out of our paychecks for unemployment insurance—like taxes.

Words to Know

laid off	employee	welfare
hired	boss	paycheck
fired	rent	taxes
seniority	apply for	_____

Another Way to Say It

I can't believe it! .... I am very surprised.

pink slip .... layoff notice

_____ .... _____

■■■■■ Talking It Over

Discuss the questions in pairs or groups.

1. Why are Mrs. Park, Mrs. Tamler, and Mr. Samuels being laid off? Do you think it's fair?
2. Why isn't Mr. Jenkins being laid off? Do you think it's fair?
3. Mrs. Tamler says, "The last one hired is the first fired." What does this mean? The workers are not really being fired. What is the difference between being fired and being laid off?
4. How do you think Mrs. Park, Mrs. Tamler, and Mr. Samuels feel? How would you feel if you were being laid off?
5. Why is Mrs. Park worried?
6. What does Mrs. Tamler plan to do?
7. Do you know people who have lost their jobs? How did they feel? What did they do?
8. In your native country, how do companies lay off workers? Are workers let go based on seniority or on the quantity or quality of the work they do?
9. What would you do if you lost your job? How would you find a new one?

Working Together

Work with your classmates and teacher to finish this conversation. Then practice with a partner.

Mrs. Park: I'm scared.

Mrs. Tamler: I know. I am, too. We'll get other jobs.

Mrs. Park: But I don't know how to find another job.

Mrs. Tamler:

Mrs. Park:

Real Talk

"Whadda ya mean?"
When a question begins with *What do you . . . ?* it is often pronounced "Whadda ya . . . ?" Listen to your teacher ask these questions:

What do you mean?	*What do you* want?
What do you do?	*What do you* think?

Superlatives

To show how something stands out among a group of three or more:

1. Add *-est* to short adjectives.

Mrs. Park is **the fastest** worker at Bonita Soups.

2. Use *most* in front of longer adjectives.

Mr. Samuels is **the most qualified** worker at Bonita Soups.

3. Use irregular adjectives: *the best* (good) and *the worst* (bad).

They are **the best** workers at Bonita Soups.

Note that the superlative form includes *the*.

Practice A

You have to hire a data-entry clerk. Describe these candidates for the job.

Mrs. Strickland
Typing Speed: 45 wpm
Experience: 17 years
Salary Requirement: $12.00
per hour

Mr. Kuroda
Typing Speed: 60 wpm
Experience: 10 months
Salary Requirement: $11.00
per hour

Miss Chi
Typing Speed: 50 wpm
Experience: 9 years
Salary Requirement: $10.00
per hour

1. (slow)

Mrs. Strickland is the slowest typist.

2. (fast)

_____

3. (high salary requirement)

_____

4. (qualified)

_____

Practice B

Write sentences about someone you know who does his or her job well.

Example: Mrs. Horvath is **the best** secretary.

She is **the fastest** worker in the company.

Read the paycheck and paycheck stub and answer the questions below.

Bonita Soups, Inc.	**105**

Date: September 30, 199__

Pay to Juan Ortega $ 1,320.96

The Amount of One thousand three hundred twenty and 96/100---------- dollars

Authorized Signature

Jerry Smith

Jerry Smith, Treasurer

For the period Sept. 1–Sept. 30

	Current	Year to Date
Regular Salary	$1,916.67	$17,249.94
Deductions		
Federal Tax	$311.67	$2,805.04
State Tax	$71.64	$644.76
FICA (Social Security)	$145.93	$1,313.35
Unemployment Insurance	$38.33	$344.97
Disability Insurance	$19.07	$171.64
Health Insurance	$9.07	$81.60

Federal Tax: Money withheld from the check and sent to the federal government to pay federal income taxes.

State Tax: Money sent to the state to pay state income taxes.

FICA (Social Security): Money put into a federal fund that pays an employee when he or she retires.

Unemployment Insurance: Money put into a state fund to pay the employee if he or she loses his or her job.

Disability Insurance: Money put into a state fund to help employees who get sick or injured and cannot work.

Health Insurance: The employer's insurance fund for workers' medical bills.

In Your Community

Find out the information individually or in groups and share it with the class.

1. Call the nearest unemployment office and ask for the procedures to collect unemployment benefits if you are laid off from your job.
2. Call the nearest Social Security office, and ask for a Request for Personal Earnings and Benefits Statement. This will tell you how much money you have in your Social Security account and what you can expect to receive when you retire.

■ ■ ■ ■ ■ Figuring Out the U.S.

As you read the passage, circle any words you don't understand and try to guess their meanings.

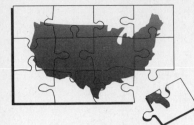

Assistance Programs

In the United States, there are programs that help you if you are unable to work. Some of the programs are paid for by the federal government. Others are paid for by city or state governments. You must follow many rules to collect money. These programs pay very little money.

1. Unemployment Benefits. You may be paid unemployment benefits if you lose your job. The amount of money you are paid depends on how long you have worked and what wage you received while you were working. Unemployment benefits are normally paid for about six months.

2. Worker's Compensation. If you are injured while you are at work, you may be paid part of your wage until you can go back to work.

3. Aid to Dependent Children. If you have young children and are poor, you may receive some money each month to help pay for food, clothing, and rent for your children.

4. Welfare. If you are very poor and do not work, you may receive welfare. This is a very small amount of money and depends on how many children you have.

5. Food Stamps. If you are poor, you may be given stamps to take to the store to buy food. You can buy only food with food stamps.

6. Medicaid. If you are poor, you may qualify for Medicaid benefits. Medicaid does not give you money. Instead, it pays doctors, hospitals, or drugstores for your health care.

Your Turn

Discuss the questions.

1. Who does worker's compensation help? What does it do?
2. Who does Medicaid help? What does it do?
3. Which programs might help you if you were poor and had children?
4. Does your native country have welfare benefits? Do you think such programs are a good idea? Why or why not?
5. The United States does not have national health care. Does your native country have a national health-care program? Do you think it is good or bad? Why?

> *Choose one of the questions and write about it.*

Before You Listen

1. Who is in the picture?
2. What is their relationship?
3. What do you think they are talking about?

■ ■ ■ ■ ■ This Is the Best Day of My Life

Listen carefully to the dialogue.

Maureen: He asked me out! This is the best day of my life! That was Timothy. He asked me to the school dance on Saturday night!

Debbie: What did you tell him?

Maureen: Why, yes, of course! He's the most mature boy in the entire school. He's smart and cute. I can't wait for Saturday night.

Debbie: Isn't that the night of the Annual All Irish Church Supper? Every year Mama spends weeks getting ready for it.

Maureen: Oh yeah, I forgot. I didn't check the calendar.

Debbie: Maureen O'Brien, you have to go to the church supper. Mama will go through the roof if you don't.

Maureen: I don't have to go. I hate those church suppers. They're so boring. Everybody talks about how wonderful Ireland is. I don't even remember Ireland. I'm not Irish. I'm American.

Debbie: Don't ever let Mama hear you say that! Religion and Ireland are two things Mama takes very seriously. Is this Timothy boy Irish?

Maureen: I don't know. He's American. I don't know what his relatives are. He was born here.

Debbie: You should call Timothy and tell him you can't go to the dance.

Maureen: I can't do that. What am I going to do? This is the worst day of my life!

Words to Know

church	cute	religion
mature	annual	relatives
entire	calendar	_____
smart	boring	_____

Another Way to Say It

asked me out .... invited me for a date

I can't wait for .... I'm very excited about

go through the roof .... become very angry, hit the ceiling

_____ ..... _____

■ ■ ■ ■ ■ Talking It Over

Discuss the questions in pairs or groups.

1. What does Maureen want to do? Why is she upset?
2. Why does Maureen want to go out with Timothy? Look back at the dialogue and find her reasons.
3. How will Maureen feel if she doesn't go to the dance with Timothy?
4. Why does Debbie think Maureen should go to the church supper? Look back at the dialogue and find her reasons.
5. Maureen feels that she is an American. She feels comfortable living in the U.S. Why is it important for a teenager to feel comfortable living in a new country?
6. Debbie says that her mother feels it is important for Maureen to be proud of her native country. Why do you think Mrs. O'Brien feels that way?

Working Together

Work with your classmates and teacher to finish this conversation. Then practice with a partner.

Maureen:	Mama, I need to ask you something.
Mrs. O'Brien:	What is it?
Maureen:	The most wonderful boy wants to take me to the school dance.
Mrs. O'Brien:	When's the dance?
Maureen:	
Mrs. O'Brien:	

Real Talk

Maureen O'Brien, you have to go to the church supper.

Americans rarely address people by both their first and last names. When they do, it is often for the purpose of making a statement stronger.

Have to/Should

Use *have to* to talk about something that must be done.

    You **have to** do your homework.

Use *don't have to* to talk about something that doesn't need to be done.

    You **don't have to** read the extra chapters.

Use *should* to indicate that it is advisable to do something.

    You **should** check your work before you hand it in.

Use *should not* or *shouldn't* to indicate that it is best not to do something.

    You **shouldn't** hand in messy homework.

Practice A

Tell Malcolm what he *has to* do and what he *should* do to the car.

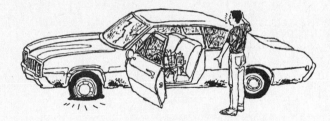

1. *You have to*   fix the flat tire.

2. _____ fix the rust spots.

3. _____ clean out the front seat.

4. _____ clean the windows.

5. _____ fix the windshield.

Practice B

Name two things you *have to* do and two things you *should* do today.

1. _____

2. _____

3. _____

4. _____

■ ■ ■ ■ ■ Read and Think

Read the community calendar carefully. Then answer the questions.

Bonita Community Calendar
Today's Events

4:30 P.M.   La Raza: Mexican-American Association Meeting. Help us plan events for the coming year.
Cummins School, Auditorium, 925 Magnolia Street

5:30 P.M.   American Legion Fried Chicken Dinner. Help us get ready for the Fourth of July Parade.
American Legion Hall, 970 Cypress Street

6:30 P.M.   Temple Shalom Business Meeting.
Temple Shalom, Main Hall, 825 Pine Street

7:00 P.M.   Korean Bible Study Group. We will be reading the Gospel According to Luke.
Rose Presbyterian Church, Fellowship Hall, 720 Rose Street

7:00 P.M.   Sons of Italy, Italian-American Club Monthly Dinner Meeting. Mario Salucci will talk about his recent trip to Italy.
Roma Nova Restaurant, 1472 State Avenue

7:30 P.M.   Bonita Historical Society. Topic: Early settlers.
Civic Association Hall, Rose Street at State Avenue

8:00 P.M.   Bonita School Board Meeting.
Redwood High School, Staff Lounge, 1510 Dixville Avenue

---

1. What's happening at the American Legion Hall tonight?
2. Which group is having a planning meeting for the coming year?
3. What time does Mario Salucci speak?
4. What will the Historical Society be discussing?
5. Where will the school board meet?

In Your Community

Find out the information individually or in groups and share it with the class.

1. Look for a community calendar in your local newspaper, and ask questions like those above.
2. What nationalities and religions are found in your city or town?
3. In your native country, are there many different religions?
4. In your native country, do people openly express their opinions about politics or religion? Why or why not?

■ ■ ■ ■ ■ Figuring Out the U.S.

This is a letter from Maureen's mother, Sharon, to a friend in Ireland. As you read her letter, circle the words you don't understand and try to guess their meanings.

A Letter to Ireland

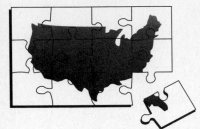

May 5

Dear Mary Cathleen,

Thank you for your letter. I'm always happy to get letters from Ireland. I will try to answer your questions about life in the U.S.

I am happy we moved to the U.S. We moved here because of the trouble in Ireland. In the U.S., we find people can have different beliefs and still live and work together.

We live in an apartment building. Some of our neighbors are Protestant. We have other neighbors who are Jewish. All of the children play together happily.

In the U.S., children have many choices. Sometimes I think there are too many choices. Maureen doesn't want to go to a church supper. She says she doesn't remember Ireland. She thinks it's old-fashioned. She says she is an American. I worry that she'll forget her roots.

I do want my daughter to fit in here. I want her to like living in America. But I also want her to be proud of Ireland.

I hope all is well with your family. Write soon.

Love,

Sharon

Your Turn

Discuss the questions.

1. Do you worship the same way in this country as you worshiped in your native country?
2. Should children participate in religious activities?
3. Is it better for children to participate in American activities or activities in America from their native countries?

> *Choose one of the questions and write about it.*

Person A

Work with a partner. Look at this page only, and your partner will look at page 20 only. Ask your partner to give you hints to help you complete the puzzle and write the words going **down**.

Number six down is written in for you. All of the words are from Chapters 1 through 3.

Example: ***Person A:*** *What's number six down?*

   Person B: *It's money people have to pay the government.*

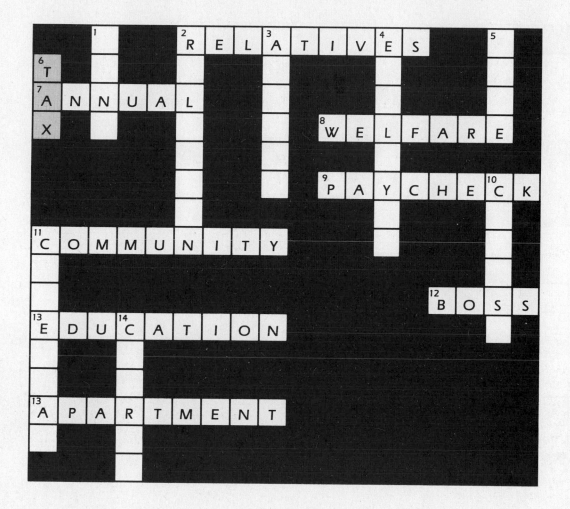

Person B

Work with a partner. Look at this page only, and your partner will look at page 19 only. Ask your partner to give you hints to help you complete the puzzle and write the words going **across**.

Number two across is written in for you. All of the words are from Chapters 1 through 3.

Example: *Person B:* What's number two across?

Person A: These are all the people in my family.

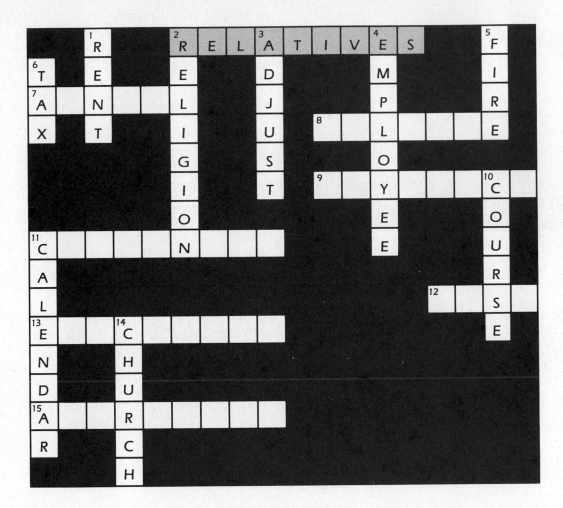

We're Having a Bad Storm

Before You Listen

1. Who is in the picture?
2. What is their relationship?
3. What's happening outside?
4. How do you think the little boy feels?
5. How do you think the woman feels?
6. Do you think Mitzy (the cat) is scared?

■ ■ ■ ■ ■ We're Having a Bad Storm

Listen carefully to the dialogue.

Mrs. Tamler: What's the matter?

Billy: Mommy, I can't sleep. Mitzy is scared. I'm scared too.

Mrs. Tamler: You don't need to be frightened. We're having a bad storm. There's nothing to worry about.

Billy: When will the noise stop?

Mrs. Tamler: It's just a thunderstorm. It sounds close, but it's really very far away. The thunder and lightning will stop soon.

Billy: What happened to the lights?

Mrs. Tamler: The power went out because of the storm. The lights won't be off very long.

Billy: Where's Daddy?

Mrs. Tamler: Daddy's bringing the bicycles in from outside. He'll come right back. Come on, I'll tuck you in.

Billy: I don't want to go back to bed. I'm scared.

Mrs. Tamler: Come sit on my lap. I'll tell you a story. When I was a little girl, we lived in a village in Turkey. We used to get terrible storms. When I was your age, we had an awful storm. . . .

Words to Know

scared	thunder	tuck in
frightened	lightning	lap
thunderstorm	power	awful

_____ _____ _____

Another Way to Say It

What's the matter? .... What's wrong?

the power went out .... the electricity turned off

come right back .... return very soon

_____ .... _____

▪▪▪▪▪ Talking It Over

Discuss the questions in pairs or groups.

1. Why did the electricity go out?
2. Why did Mr. Tamler go outside? Was it safe for him to go outside?
3. Why is Billy scared? Look back at the dialogue and find his reasons.
4. Mrs. Tamler doesn't seem scared. Why isn't she scared? Look back at the dialogue to find her reasons.
5. Do you think she has other reasons? What might they be?
6. When you were a child, what things frightened you?
7. When you got scared as a child, who would help you?
8. How can you help children when they are frightened?
9. Do earthquakes, floods, hurricanes, droughts, or other natural disasters happen in your area?
10. Do any natural disasters happen in your native country?
11. What should you do if your electricity or telephone goes out?

Working Together

Work with your classmates and teacher to finish this conversation. Then practice with a partner.

Mr. Tamler: I thought Mommy told you to go back to bed.
Billy: Yeah, but I'm still scared.
Mr. Tamler:
Billy:

Real Talk

$Mommy \rightarrow Mom \qquad Daddy \rightarrow Dad \qquad Billy \rightarrow Bill$

Young children often call their mother *Mommy*. When they get older, they call her *Mom*. They often call their father *Daddy*, and when they grow older they shorten the name to *Dad*. This is often true of children's first names. When he grows older, for example, *Billy* will probably be called *Bill*.

What other familiar names have you heard children use to address their parents? What nicknames have you heard?

> **Wh-Questions**
>
> Wh-questions begin with a question word such as:
> Who   What   When   Where   Why   How
> Use wh-questions to get specific information.
>
> **Who** was there?   **When** did it happen?
> **What** happened?   **Where** did it happen?
>   **Why** did it happen?
>   **How** did it happen?

Practice A

There was a terrible fire. Birna, a reporter, talked to fire fighter Regules about the fire. Look at his answers and write the questions Birna asked.

1. *Who started the fire?*
   No one knows who started the fire.

2. _____
   The fire was in the Gibson apartment.

3. _____
   It started at about 1:00 this morning.

4. _____
   Someone started the fire by smoking in bed.

5. _____
   The Lopezes, the Gibsons, and the Engs were inside.

6. _____
   They climbed out of the building.

7. _____
   Mrs. Lopez was hurt. But the doctors say she'll be just fine.

Practice B

Think of an emergency that happened recently in your community. Work with a partner. One person is a rescue worker. The other is a reporter. The reporter asks the rescue worker questions about the emergency. *Practice* A shows one way to start.

■■■■■ Read and Think

Read the news report and try to guess the meanings of the underlined words. Rephrase each paragraph. Then answer the questions.

News Update

Keep your radio <u>tuned</u> to 89.5 AM. This is your all news–all weather station. The latest news in Bonita. This is a KCLC news <u>update</u>.

Today's high winds and heavy rain caused <u>severe damage</u>. Many trees and power lines were knocked down in the Dixville and Walnut Canyon areas. Police have closed these areas to all <u>traffic</u> except for <u>emergency vehicles</u>. The power company tells us that 2,000 homes and businesses in the Oak Hills area will be without power for at least 48 hours.

We have many <u>cancellations</u> today because of the weather. Cypress General Hospital has canceled the Well-Baby Clinic for the rest of the week. Classes in all Bonita public schools are canceled as well as all evening classes at Bonita Community College. Stay tuned for other school <u>closings</u>.

Now for the latest weather. The storm will end in a few hours. This evening we will have <u>cloudy</u> skies. Tomorrow we should have clear, sunny skies: the high temperature will be 61 degrees; the low should be about 41.

1. Why are the schools closed in Bonita?
2. Why are people without power?
3. When will the storm end?

In Your Community

Find out the information individually or in groups and share it with the class.

1. Find out how local schools and clinics notify people of cancellations. Is there a telephone number to call? Do local radio and television stations announce school closings? Which stations?
2. Many parts of the U.S. have severe weather or tornado *watches* and *warnings*. How do you prepare for severe weather or tornadoes?
3. How does the Red Cross help people in case of a natural disaster in your area? How can you find out about other relief agencies in your community?

■■■■■ Figuring Out the U.S.

As you read about newspaper headlines, circle the words you don't understand and try to guess their meanings.

The *Bonita Gazette*

The *Bonita Gazette* has these sections or columns:

Local News	Sports
National News	Advice
International News	Weather
Business	Classified Ads

Here are some headlines from the *Bonita Gazette*. In which section would you look for each article? Example:

India Holds National Elections ___*International News*___

1. Storm Causes Bonita Schools to Close _____

2. Help Wanted, Part-Time _____

3. Wife Can't Understand Mother-in-Law _____

4. Tomorrow Will Be Sunny and Warm _____

5. More Banks Report Money Problems _____

6. Giants Beat Red Sox 10–8 _____

7. Congress Votes More Money for Education _____

Your Turn

Discuss the questions.

1. Are some U.S. newspapers easier to read than others? Why? Which are easier? Which are more difficult?
2. Which one is your favorite newspaper? What section of the newspaper do you like best?
3. Is news from your native country reported in U.S. newspapers? Are sports events from your native country reported in U.S. newspapers?
4. Compare newspapers in the U.S. to newspapers in your native country. Do newspapers in the U.S. have more or less international news?

> *Choose one of the questions and write about it.*

You're Watching "Our Community"

Before You Listen

1. Where are these people?
2. Are they agreeing with each other?
3. What do you think they're talking about?
4. What is *community television*?

■ ■ ■ ■ ■ You're Watching "Our Community"

Listen carefully to the dialogue.

Ms. Lin: Hello. You're watching "Our Community," a current events TV show. My name is Tracy Lin, and I'm your host. Today we have a controversial topic: printing election ballots in many languages. I'm happy to welcome Mr. O'Brien from the English-Only Committee and Mrs. Romero from the Hispanic-American League. Let's start with Mr. O'Brien.

Mr. O'Brien: Yes. Thank you. We want ballots printed only in English.

Mrs. Romero: But U.S. citizens speak many languages. If ballots are printed only in English, lots of citizens won't understand them.

Mr. O'Brien: People should learn to speak English well if they are becoming United States citizens.

Mrs. Romero: People should vote if they become U.S. citizens. And they can't vote if they can't read the ballot.

Mr. O'Brien: Mrs. Romero, I agree. But they have to learn to read English. This is their new country, and the language here is English.

Ms. Lin: The language on ballots is really hard to understand. Ballot propositions are confusing even for native English speakers.

Mrs. Romero: Yes, Proposition J was very confusing. If you wanted state offices to close on Friday afternoons, you voted *no*. If you didn't want them to close, you had to vote *yes*!

Mr. O'Brien: Well, I still say. . . .

Words to Know

ballots	citizen	proposition
vote	election	confusing
_____	_____	_____

Another Way to Say It

current events .... news
lots of .... many
_____ .... _____

■■■■■ Talking It Over

Discuss the questions in pairs or groups.

1. What is the topic of the television show?
2. What does the English-Only Committee want?
3. What does the Hispanic-American League want?
4. Why does Mr. O'Brien think ballots should be printed only in English? Look back at the dialogue and find his reasons.
5. Why does Mrs. Romero think ballots should be printed in other languages? Look back at the dialogue and find her reasons.
6. Why do you think Mr. O'Brien says he agrees with Mrs. Romero?
7. In your native country, in what language(s) are ballots printed?
8. Are the propositions hard to understand even in your native language?
9. In what language(s) do you think ballots in the U.S. should be printed?
10. Do you have cable television programs like this in your community? What topics are discussed?

Working Together

Work with your classmates to prepare for a discussion.

1. As a class, brainstorm a list of controversial topics that could be discussed on community television programs.
2. In groups of three, select one of these topics. (You may want to talk about teenagers and drinking or raising taxes to pay for education.) One person will play the role of the television show's host, and the other two people will argue the two sides of the issue.

Real Talk

Yes. Thank you. We believe that ballots should. . . .

Well, I still say. . . .

Yes and *well* are used as conversation fillers when the next speaker needs more time to answer a question or to think about what was just said.

What other words do you hear people use as fillers? Make a list.

If/Then

If/then describes a possible condition and the result.

    If ballots are printed only in English,
[**then**] lots of citizens won't understand
them.

Then is often omitted, especially in informal
spoken English.

You can also reverse the order of the
condition and the result.

    And they can't vote **if** they can't read the ballot.

Practice A

Look back at the dialogue. Write three *if/then* sentences from the dialogue
that you agree with.

1. _____

2. _____

3. _____

Practice B

Now rewrite the three sentences, and reverse the order of the condition and
the result.

1. _____

2. _____

3. _____

Practice C

Work with a partner to prepare for a class debate on the English-only issue.
Use *if/then* sentences such as the ones you chose for *Practice* A and your
own ideas to support your argument. (Remember that in a debate someone
often has to argue an idea he or she doesn't necessarily agree with.)

▪▪▪▪▪ Read and Think

Read the television listings for Saturday, and try to guess the meanings of any words you don't understand. Then answer the questions.

TV Highlights

Check your daily paper for last-minute changes. [R] means rerun.

Noon (3)	**Movie: Gigi**, 1958—Maurice Chevalier stars in this Academy Award–winning film.
2:00 P.M. (9)	**Nature**—Scientist helps save the bald eagle from extinction.
3:00 P.M. (7)	***Our Town**—School superintendent Robert Hsu and school board member Rubén Jimenez discuss Bonita Public Schools budget problems.
3:00 P.M. (4)	**Professional Bowling**—[Tape] Semifinals.
3:30 P.M. (8)	**Gourmet Time**—Chef Lynda Norkosky prepares a chocolate layer cake.
4:05 P.M. (9)	**Baseball**—[Live] San Francisco Giants at New York Mets.
5:30 P.M. (27)	**High School Basketball**—[Tape] North High Eagles vs. the record-holding Central High Astros.
8:00 P.M. (3)	**Houston**—[R] Reginald buys oil company from his bankrupt ex-wife, Keith leaves Anna. Adult drama.
9:30 P.M. (7)	**Army Hospital**—[R] J.B. and Falconi get in trouble for hoarding scarce supplies. Antiwar comedy.

*This is broadcast simultaneously in Spanish on 99.7 FM and in Cantonese on 94 FM.

---

1. What programs are reruns?
2. What programs might be interesting for children?
3. Is the baseball game being played in San Francisco or New York?
4. Which programs would you watch if you had a teenager?
5. How would you listen to "Our Town" in Cantonese?

In Your Community

Find out this information individually or in groups and share it with the class.

1. Using a television listing from the newspaper, decide which programs and how much television children should be allowed to watch.
2. Find out what television services are broadcast in your community. Are any programs broadcast in other languages? What cable services are available? How much do they cost?
3. Keep a log of television programs your family watches for a week. What types of programs are most popular: news, sports, dramas? Are these programs in English? Share your logs with your classmates.

As you read about TV advertising, circle the words you don't understand and try to guess their meanings.

Watch Television; Watch Your Wallet

Most television programs in the U.S. are paid for by commercial advertisements. These commercials encourage the viewer to buy something by describing a product. Commercials also give the impression that if people use the product, they will be smarter, happier, or more attractive.

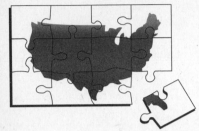

Public television stations usually do not have commercials. Public television gets operating money from the government, from corporations and foundations, and from its viewers. Public television stations often have pledge drives that encourage people to promise to give money to the station to keep it operating.

Most commercials last between 15 seconds and a minute and are shown during television programs. The type of product that is advertised during a television program depends on the type of program being shown. For instance, there are beer ads during sports programs because some people like to drink beer while watching sports events on TV. There are ads for children's cereals and toys during children's programs. These commercials try to get children to ask their parents to buy their products.

Some companies use 900 numbers, telephone numbers that begin with 900, in their advertisements. When you dial a 900 number, you are charged by the minute for the call. You pay not only for the product you order; you also pay for the telephone call to order it!

Your Turn

Discuss the questions.

1. Do television programs in your native country have commercials?
2. What are your favorite commercials? What are your least favorite commercials? Why?
3. Have you had an experience with a 900 number? What happened?
4. Have you ever bought anything that was advertised on television? Did the product do everything the commercial said it would do?

> *Choose one of the questions and write about it.*

Before You Listen

1. Where are these people?
2. Do they know each other?
3. What do you think they are talking about?
4. Where do you think they are going?

■■■■■ I Checked Out This Book

Listen carefully to the dialogue.

Mr. Samuels: Hi, Mrs. Park.

Mrs. Park: Oh, hi, Mr. Samuels. I haven't seen you since we were laid off. How are you?

Mr. Samuels: Fine thanks, except I haven't found a job yet. It's really frustrating. Have you found anything?

Mrs. Park: No, I haven't found a job either.

Mr. Samuels: You haven't found a job? I was sure you'd get one in no time!

Mrs. Park: I'm really worried. I've answered all the ads in the newspaper. I was offered one job, but the pay wasn't even enough to pay for child care. So I turned it down.

Mr. Samuels: Have you called Bonita Soups? Maybe they're hiring again.

Mrs. Park: Yes, I have. But there's nothing yet.

Mr. Samuels: I've called every single company in the area. I haven't even had one job interview. I'm worried too.

Mrs. Park: I just went to the library to look for a job.

Mr. Samuels: You want a job as a librarian?

Mrs. Park: No. The library has a job resource center. It has information on jobs that I've never thought of.

Mr. Samuels: Like what?

Mrs. Park: Well, I checked out this book called *Careers in Education.* . . .

Words to Know

checked out	interview	resource center
frustrating	librarian	careers
_____	_____	_____

Another Way to Say It

turned it down .... refused it

every single company .... all the companies

_____ .... _____

■ ■ ■ ■ ■ Talking It Over

Discuss the questions in pairs or groups.

1. Why are Mr. Samuels and Mrs. Park worried?
2. What did Mr. Samuels do to find a job?
3. What did Mrs. Park do to find a job? Why did she go to the library?
4. What else could they do to find jobs?
5. Why didn't Mrs. Park accept the job she was offered?
6. Why do you think Mrs. Park checked out the book *Careers in Education*?
7. What could Mrs. Park and Mr. Samuels do to save money until they find another job?
8. Have you ever turned down a job because it didn't cover the cost of child care? How much do you have to pay for child care?
9. In your native country, what do people do if they are out of work for a long time?

Working Together

Work with your classmates and teacher to finish this conversation. Then practice with a partner.

Mrs. Park: I'm looking for books about job training programs. Where would I find them?

Librarian: What kind of job training program do you want?

Mrs. Park: Well, I'm not sure.

Librarian: Hmmm. . . . What do you like to do?

Mrs. Park:

Librarian:

Real Talk

Many statements can be turned into questions by using rising intonation. Listen to your teacher ask these questions:

<u>You haven't found a / job?</u> *(I was sure you'd get one in no time!)*

<u>You want a job as a li / brarian?</u>

Present Perfect

The present perfect uses *have* and the past participle to describe an action that began in the past and continues into the present.

    I **have answered** all the ads in the newspaper.

The two parts of the verb are separated in questions and negative statements.

    Have you **found** anything?

    No, I **haven't found** a job either.

Short answers are: Yes, I have. No, I haven't.

Practice

Mrs. Rogers, personnel manager for the Bonita Department of Public Works, is interviewing Mr. Samuels for a job. Complete the conversation, using one of the following words in each space. You may choose the same word twice.

had	worked	driven	used	have	haven't

Mrs. Rogers: I need to know what skills you have, Mr. Samuels. Have you ever _____ a truck?

Mr. Samuels: Yes, I _____. I drove a delivery truck for Bonita Soups.

Mrs. Rogers: Have you _____ a vehicle with a stick shift?

Mr. Samuels: No, I _____. My delivery truck had an automatic shift.

Mrs. Rogers: Have you _____ in an office?

Mr. Samuels: Yes, I _____. I worked as a copy machine operator at Knox Paper Company.

Mrs. Rogers: _____ you _____ a word processor?

Mr. Samuels: No, I _____.

■ ■ ■ ■ ■ Read and Think

Read the library pamphlet and try to guess the meanings of the underlined words. Rephrase each paragraph.

JOB RESOURCE CENTER

Looking for a job? The Bonita Public Library has many <u>resources</u> to help you with your job search.

Newspapers and Magazines
The library receives more than 50 magazines and newspapers every month with listings for hundreds of job openings.

Job Resource Books
The Bonita Public Library has a <u>collection</u> of job resource books. We have books that tell about specific job fields such as careers in medicine or banking. Other books suggest ways to look for jobs.

Telephone Directories
The library has <u>telephone directories</u> for the entire state. We have both the white and yellow pages. <u>Job hunters</u> often check the addresses and telephone numbers of possible employers before they send in a letter or go to a job interview.

Job Training Program Catalogs
The Bonita Library has catalogs for many job training programs. These programs may be at <u>technical</u> schools or be a part of colleges or <u>universities</u>.

In Your Community

Find out the information individually or in groups and share it with the class. Call or visit your local library.

1. Where is the library? When is it open?
2. How do you get a library card?
3. What materials does it have in addition to books?
4. How long can you keep books? How long can you keep other materials? How much does the library charge for overdue books?
5. Does the library have materials in other languages? Which ones?
6. Does it have special services for children? Does it have a children's room? Does it have toys?

■ ■ ■ ■ ■ Figuring Out the U.S.

As you read the passage, circle the words you don't understand and try to guess their meanings.

Libraries Are the Perfect Family Place

People in the U.S. place a very high value on reading. Libraries are free. It doesn't cost anything to have a library card or to check out books. They are paid for by the government and by donations.

Libraries have more than just books. They often have magazines, newspapers, maps, pamphlets, audiotapes, videotapes, records, CDs, and computers and software. Librarians help people find what they need.

Libraries often organize community activities. There may be lectures about the history of the community or clubs about topics such as investments and gardening.

Adults who cannot read in their own language or who need to learn another language can sometimes get training at the local library. There are national organizations in the U.S. that promote adult literacy through local libraries.

Many libraries have a children's room and story hours for children. During story hour, children listen to a book read to them out loud. It's important for children to like to read if they want to do well in school.

Libraries have something for everyone in the family!

Your Turn

Discuss the questions.

1. Why do you think libraries are an important part of U.S. culture?
2. Why is it important for people to read?
3. Is there a literacy program in your native country?
4. What do you like to read? What do people in your family like to read?

> *Choose one of the questions and write about it.*

At the Library

Person A

Work with a partner. Look at this page only, and your partner will look at page 40 only.

You and your partner have the same diagram of the Bonita Public Library. You need to find some things in the library that are marked on your partner's diagram but not on yours. First ask your partner where to find these things:

The card catalog   A computer software program

The *New York Times*   A detective novel

A children's story   Book check out

Write on your diagram where to find each thing. Then help your partner find the things he or she needs.

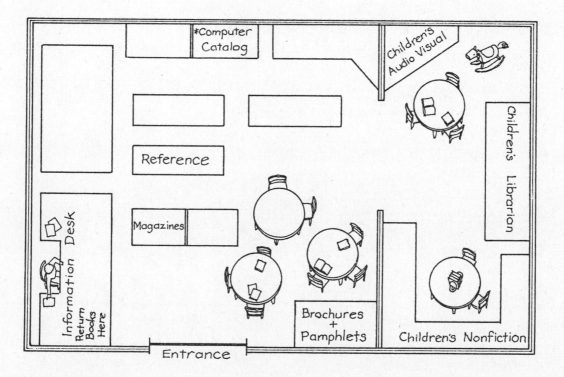

*A *computer catalog* is a computerized card catalog.

At the Library

Person B

Work with a partner. Look at this page only, and your partner will look at page 39 only.

You and your partner have the same diagram of the Bonita Public Library. You need to find some things in the Library that are marked on your partner's diagram but not on yours. First help your partner find the things he or she needs. Then ask your partner where to find these things:

The computer catalog
(Computerized card catalog)

An English/Spanish dictionary

A catalog for Bonita Community College

Time magazine

Book returns

A children's video

Write on your diagram where to find each thing.

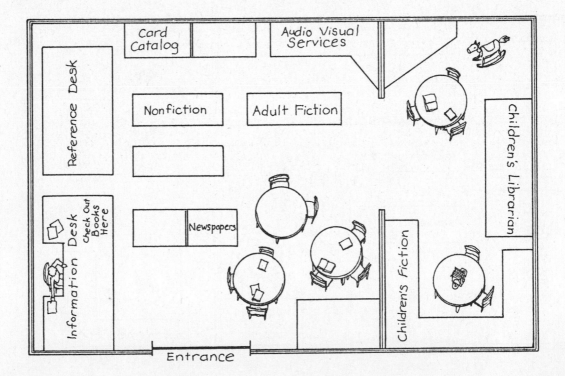

I'm So Tired!

Before You Listen

1. Who are these people?
2. What do you think Grandmother Cogam has been doing?
3. Does she look tired?
4. What do you think Ruth has been doing?
5. Does she look tired?

■■■■■ I'm So Tired!

Listen carefully to the dialogue.

Ruth: Hi, Grandmother. How was your exercise class?

Grandmother: It was great. You should take a class. The Parks and Recreation Department has a fitness program for teenagers.

Ruth: I can't even think about an exercise class. I'm so tired! I can hardly move.

Grandmother: You wouldn't be so tired if you exercised.

Ruth: That doesn't make any sense. I'm too tired to exercise. I had a very long day. I had school until three. After school, I worked at Fred's Market. Then, I came home, studied, and took care of the baby.

Grandmother: When I got to class this afternoon, I was pooped. I had a long morning too. First, I took care of your baby sister. Then, I took her to the doctor. After that, I cleaned the house and did the laundry.

Ruth: And then you went to an exercise class?

Grandmother: Yeah. When I got there, I was really tired. After we started working out, I began to feel better. Now I feel great. Think about taking a fitness class.

Ruth: I suppose now you'll tell me I should eat healthier food.

Grandmother: Well, you shouldn't eat so much junk food.

Ruth: Oh, Grandmother. . . .

Words to Know

exercise	fitness	laundry
recreation	pooped	_____

Another Way to Say It

can hardly move .... can move only a little
working out .... exercising
junk food .... unhealthy food

■■■■■ Talking It Over

Discuss the questions in pairs or groups.

1. How does Grandmother Cogam feel about exercise?
2. How does Ruth feel about exercise?
3. Do you think people are more tired or less tired after they exercise?
4. What types of exercise do you think people do in the U.S.?
5. What types of exercise do people do in your native country?
6. How do people in your native country feel about exercise?
7. Do you exercise? Why or why not?
8. If you do exercise, what do you do?

Working Together

You should get medical advice before you begin an exercise program or go on a diet. The people listed below want to begin an exercise program or lose weight. In small groups, list questions each of these people could ask his or her doctor or health-care professional.

1. Ms. Lukac is 60 years old. She has high blood pressure. She wants to start an exercise program.
2. Mr. Sin-La is 28 years old. He is not overweight. He smokes. He wants to be healthier.
3. Mrs. Miranda is 30 years old. She is five feet tall and weighs 200 pounds. She wants to lose weight.

Real Talk

When Ruth disagrees with her grandmother in the dialogue, she challenges her logic by saying, "That doesn't make any sense." She could also say:

> *I'm not sure about that.*
>
> *I don't know about that.*

These are more polite ways to disagree with someone. Can you think of any other polite expressions that Americans use to disagree with someone?

Time Clauses

Use a time clause to tell when something happens or to tell the order in which things happened.

Before I went to class, I cleaned the house.

When I got to class this afternoon, I was pooped.

After we started working out, I began to feel better.

A time clause is not a complete sentence. It cannot stand alone.

Practice A

These people were very busy this morning. Combine these sentences to tell what they did. Use time clauses.

1. Mrs. Cogam washed the clothes. She did the ironing.

After she washed the clothes,
she did the ironing.

2. We exercised for half an hour. We swam in the pool.

_____

_____

3. Ruth opened the door. She dropped the whole stack of books.

_____

_____

4. The cat ran into the street. I stopped my car.

_____

_____

Practice B

Finish these sentences with your own information. Then create your own sentences using time clauses. Discuss them with a partner.

1. Before I left my native country, _____.

2. When I came to the U.S., _____.

■■■■■ Read and Think

Read the pamphlets for the public parks and recreation program and the private health club. Try to guess the meanings of the words you don't understand. Then tell which program you would like to join.

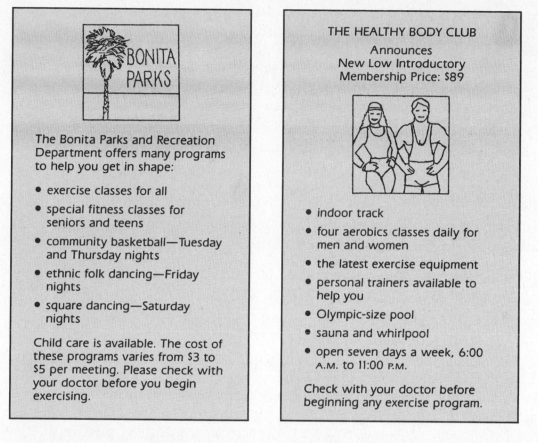

BONITA PARKS

The Bonita Parks and Recreation Department offers many programs to help you get in shape:

- exercise classes for all
- special fitness classes for seniors and teens
- community basketball—Tuesday and Thursday nights
- ethnic folk dancing—Friday nights
- square dancing—Saturday nights

Child care is available. The cost of these programs varies from $3 to $5 per meeting. Please check with your doctor before you begin exercising.

THE HEALTHY BODY CLUB
Announces
New Low Introductory
Membership Price: $89

- indoor track
- four aerobics classes daily for men and women
- the latest exercise equipment
- personal trainers available to help you
- Olympic-size pool
- sauna and whirlpool
- open seven days a week, 6:00 A.M. to 11:00 P.M.

Check with your doctor before beginning any exercise program.

In Your Community

Find out the information individually or in groups and share it with the class.

Prepare to call or visit your local Parks and Recreation Department, the YMCA/YWCA, and health clubs. Make a list of questions you want to ask. Start with these questions and add your own. Be sure to get pamphlets about the programs.

1. What types of programs do you offer?
2. Are there separate programs for men and women?
3. Are there special programs for senior citizens or pregnant women?

▪▪▪▪▪ Figuring Out the U.S.

As you read the passage, circle the words you don't understand and try to guess their meanings.

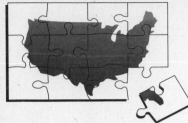

Let's Get Healthy!

Some people in the U.S. take their health very seriously. They watch what they eat and drink. They try to stay thin and in good shape. And they are also quitting smoking.

Healthy Foods Are More Popular

People in the U.S. are not eating as many junk foods— foods that have a lot of fat, salt, or sugar. Doctors say it is important to eat healthy foods. They say we should eat a variety of foods every day.

Alcohol Consumption Is Down

Statistics show that people are drinking less alcohol. Drinking too much can harm your liver and other important organs. Alcohol can also hurt a family in other ways. Living with an alcoholic is very hard on a family.

People Are Getting in Shape

Many people believe that if you exercise several times a week, you will live longer and be healthier. It is very common to see people of all ages jogging or in exercise classes.

No Smoking Is Becoming Common

On airplanes that fly within the U.S., it is illegal to smoke on flights less than four hours long. In many restaurants and other public places, it is also against the law to smoke. Smoking is known to cause lung cancer and other lung diseases.

Your Turn

Discuss the questions.

1. Why are people in the U.S. quitting smoking and drinking?
2. Why are people in the U.S. getting in shape?
3. How do people in your native country feel about drinking and smoking?
4. What do you consider to be a healthy diet? How is your diet?
5. What do you think someone should do to be healthy?

> *Choose one of the questions and write about it.*

I Can't Be Late for Work!

Before You Listen

1. Where are these people?
2. Why are they stopped?
3. Why do you think Mr. Samuels is upset?
4. Why do you think Mrs. Samuels is upset?

■■■■■ I Can't Be Late for Work!

Listen carefully to the dialogue.

Mrs. Samuels: I'm so mad that the car has broken down again! This car isn't a form of transportation. It's just a headache.

Mr. Samuels: Try to start it now.

Mrs. Samuels: Why won't it start? It has to start. I have to get to work on time!

Mr. Samuels: It almost started. It could be the starter. Or it could be the battery. Maybe it's just the cable.

Mrs. Samuels: I can't stand it when this happens.

Mr. Samuels: Try it just one more time.

Mrs. Samuels: Oh no! What's that smoke?

Mr. Samuels: It's not smoke; it's steam.

Mrs. Samuels: I can't believe this!

Mr. Samuels: Let me see if I can fix it.

Mrs. Samuels: What am I going to do? I can't be late for work!

Mr. Samuels: I could call your boss and tell him you'll be late.

Mrs. Samuels: No! Don't do that! If you call him, then the whole store will know I'm late. Could I walk?

Mr. Samuels: No. It's too far.

Mrs. Samuels: Oh, what can I do?

Words to Know

transportation	battery	smoke
headache	cable	steam

_____ _____ _____

Another Way to Say It

broken down .... stopped working
I can't stand it .... I get very upset

_____ ....

■■■■■ Talking It Over

Discuss the questions in pairs or groups.

1. What happened to the Samuels' car?
2. Do you think this has happened before? Why or why not?
3. What is Mr. Samuels trying to do?
4. Why doesn't Mrs. Samuels want Mr. Samuels to call her boss?
5. What do you think Mrs. Samuels did in the end?
6. What are the advantages of owning a car?
7. What are the advantages of using public transportation?
8. Do you own a car?
9. How do you get to class?
10. Do you use public transportation? Why or why not?

Working Together

Mrs. Samuels could ride the bus to work if she can find out which bus to take. She has to call the bus hot line. Practice this telephone conversation with a partner. Then use your own information.

Mrs. Samuels: Hello. I need to go downtown to the corner of Washington and Pine. I'm out on Dixville Avenue now. Which bus should I take?

Clerk: You need to take number 56.

Mrs. Samuels: How much is the bus fare?

Clerk: $1.25. And you need exact change.

Mrs. Samuels: Thank you. Good-bye.

Real Talk

Oh no! What's that smoke?

Oh no! is used to show strong negative feelings. Someone who is very angry, afraid, or disappointed might say, "Oh no!" In the dialogue, *Oh no!* is used to express disappointment.

Could

Use *could* to suggest possible alternatives. Use *could* with the simple form of the verb.

    It **could** be the starter. Or it **could** be the battery.

For yes/no questions, use *could* at the beginning of the sentence.

    Could I walk?

Practice A

Read the calendar and make suggestions for what you could do in Bonita on Saturday. Write them on the lines below. Follow the example.

Bonita Community Calendar

Saturday

8:00 A.M.	3-Mile Walk to Help End Homelessness
9:30 A.M.	Temple Shalom Annual Cleanup Day
10:00 A.M.	St. Patrick's Church Annual Rummage Sale
11:00 A.M.	Little League Baseball Parade
12:00 noon	Bonita Town Picnic
2:00 P.M.	Friends of the Library Book Sale
7:30 P.M.	Square Dancing: Come and square dance.
8:00 P.M.	Bonita Community Sing: Come and sing.

---

1. *I could watch the baseball parade.*

2. _____

3. _____

4. _____

Practice B

Work with a partner. Ask questions and give alternatives about what you could do in your community this weekend.

Example: ***Person A:*** *Could I go to the library on Saturday?*
            Person B: *Yes. Or you could go to the baseball game.*

The O'Briens are going to visit their family in New York, Washington, D.C., and Boston. Read the train schedule and answer the questions.

Understanding a Train Schedule

East Coast Railway Southbound Service				East Coast Railway Northbound Service			
Train Number	**111***	**119**	**128**	**Train Number**	**211***	**219**	**228**
Depart Boston	6:30	10:20	1:35	Depart Wash. D.C.	7:20	11:20	3:20
Arrive New York Depart New York	11:06 11:20	2:56 3:11	6:10 6:35	Arrive Phila. Depart Phila.	9:05 9:08	1:10 1:13	5:15 5:20
Arrive Phila. Depart Phila.	12:39 12:42	4:59 5:04	7:56 7:59	Arrive New York Depart New York	10:39 10:43	2:47 3:06	6:40 7:11
Arrive Wash. D.C.	2:42	7:10	9:59	Arrive Boston	3:49	7:48	11:59

Train schedule subject to change without notice.
Shaded area is P.M.
*No service Sundays or holidays.

1. If the O'Briens wanted to go from New York to Washington, D.C., in the morning, which train could they take? (Use the train number in your answer.) When would they leave New York? When would they arrive in Washington, D.C.?
2. If the O'Briens wanted to go from Washington to Boston on Sunday, which trains could they take? When would they leave Washington? When would they arrive in Boston?
3. If the O'Briens wanted to go from Boston to Washington, D.C., in the evening, which train could they take? When would they leave Boston? When would they arrive in Washington, D.C.?

In Your Community

Find out the information about public transportation individually or in groups and share it with the class. Look in the yellow pages of your telephone directory under Railroads *and* Transit Lines *to find buses, taxis, trains, and subways.*

1. What types of public transportation are available within your community? Does your community have subways or trains? How much does it cost to ride? Where do they go?
2. What types of public transportation are available from your city to other cities close by? What's the fastest form of transportation? What's the least expensive form of transportation?

▪▪▪▪▪ Figuring Out the U.S.

As you read the pamphlet, circle the words you don't understand and try to guess their meanings.

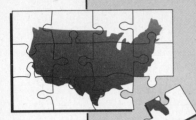

BTA
Bonita Transit Authority

General Information

Buses run daily from 5:00 A.M. to midnight.* Please call 555-3230 for exact schedule and fares. Transfers are available.

Monthly passes are available at 30% discount. Passes may be purchased at the Bonita Bus Terminal.

Senior citizens over 62 pay half fare. Show your senior citizen card as you board the bus.

Students 6–18 pay half fare. Show your student ID as you board the bus.

Children 5 and under ride free.

*Buses do not operate on Thanksgiving or Christmas.

Special Services

Services for the Disabled: A van equipped for wheelchairs runs between 8:00 A.M. and 6:00 P.M. For more information, please call 555-ABLE.

Car Pools: For information on starting up or joining a car pool, please call 555-2348.

Airport Service: Buses from Bonita Bus Terminal to the airport run every hour on the hour from 7:00 A.M. to 10:00 P.M. Buses pick up at Terminal C every hour on the half hour from 7:30 A.M. to 10:30 P.M. The trip takes 25 minutes.

Your Turn

Discuss the questions.

1. Do you have good public transportation in your community?
2. What special fares are available for your local public transportation?
3. How could public transportation in your community be improved?
4. What is public transportation like in your native country?
5. How does public transportation in your community compare to public transportation in your native country?

> *Choose one of the questions and write about it.*

9 | Can You Please Help Me?

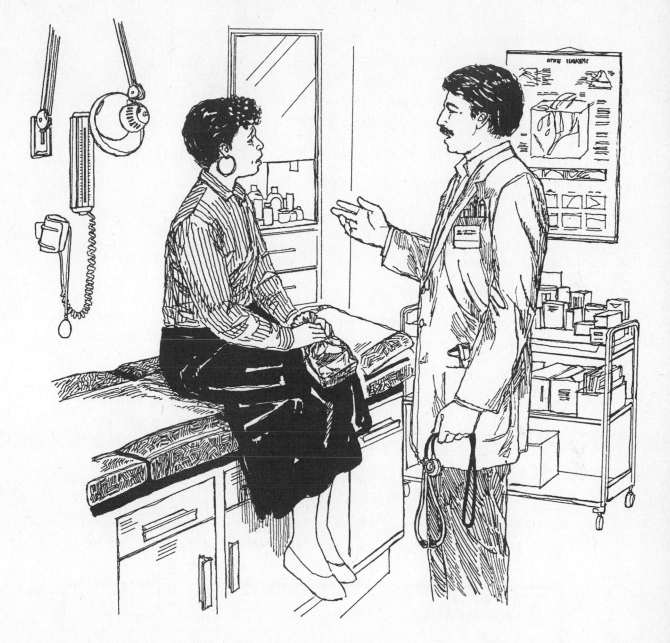

Before You Listen

1. Who are these people?
2. Where are they?
3. Why do you think Mrs. Romero is in the emergency room?
4. Why do you think she is holding a paper bag?

■■■■■ Can You Please Help Me?

Listen carefully to the dialogue.

Mrs. Romero: I can't breathe! I'm going to die! Can you please help me?

Dr. Shanmugan: You're not going to die! Try to calm down. You're taking in too much air. I want you to breathe slowly in and out of this paper bag.

Mrs. Romero: I'm beginning to feel better already.

Dr. Shanmugan: Has this ever happened to you before?

Mrs. Romero: Yes, but I've kept it to myself. I was afraid people would think I'm going crazy. It's really awful.

Dr. Shanmugan: Why did you come to the emergency room today?

Mrs. Romero: It keeps getting worse.

Dr. Shanmugan: How often does this happen to you?

Mrs. Romero: Oh, about once or twice a week. Every time it happens, it gets worse. Doctor, what's wrong with me?

Dr. Shanmugan: Your heart is fine. Your blood pressure is OK. I think you've been having panic attacks. I'd like you to make an appointment to see a therapist at the mental health clinic.

Mrs. Romero: Mental health clinic? That's for crazy people. Do you think I'm off my rocker?

Dr. Shanmugan: No, I don't. But I do think you need some counseling. They can help you at the mental health clinic.

Words to Know

breathe	therapist	therapy
emergency room	mental health clinic	crazy
panic attacks	counseling	_____

Another Way to Say It

kept it to myself .... didn't tell anyone

off my rocker .... insane

■■■■■ Talking It Over

Discuss the questions in pairs or groups.

1. Why did Mrs. Romero go to the emergency room?
2. What did Dr. Shanmugan say was wrong with Mrs. Romero?
3. How did Mrs. Romero feel about it?
4. Why did the doctor tell Mrs. Romero to visit the mental health clinic?
5. Why didn't Mrs. Romero want to visit the clinic?
6. Should Mrs. Romero get counseling? Why or why not?
7. Have you ever seen anyone have a panic attack? If so, what happened?
8. Where do people in your native country get help for emotional or psychological problems? Who do they talk to?

Working Together

Work with your classmates and teacher to finish this conversation. Then practice with a partner.

Dr. Shanmugan: Why don't you want to go to the mental health clinic?
  Mrs. Romero: They can't do anything.
Dr. Shanmugan:
  Mrs. Romero:

Real Talk

I want you to breathe slowly in and out of this paper bag.
I'd like you to make an appointment to see a therapist.

Dr. Shanmugan gives Mrs. Romero specific instructions. They might look more like requests than orders when you read them.

However, they are orders because Dr. Shanmugan is the doctor. People usually follow "doctor's orders" faithfully in the United States. Should she follow the doctor's orders?

Reported Speech: Present Tense

Use *says* to report what someone has just said. Do not use quotation marks.

      The doctor **says** [that] Mrs. Romero **is having** a panic attack.

In informal spoken English, *that* is usually omitted.

Practice A

Read these tributes to Elena Romero.

Elena Romero is an outspoken champion for bilingual ballots.
            —Tracy Lin, KWIN-TV

Elena has helped many people at the Hispanic-American League. Bonita is a better place because of Elena.   —Ralph Vallente, mayor of Bonita

Elena is such a good daughter. Elena makes sure I am never lonely.
            —Elena's mother

What nice things do people say about Mrs. Romero? Write three sentences.

    Example: *Elena's mother says Elena is such a good daughter.*

1. _____

2. _____

3. _____

Practice B

What nice things do people say about you? Write three sentences.

    Example: *Everyone says that I am very kind.*

1. _____

2. _____

3. _____

■■■■■ Read and Think

Read the pamphlet and answer the questions.

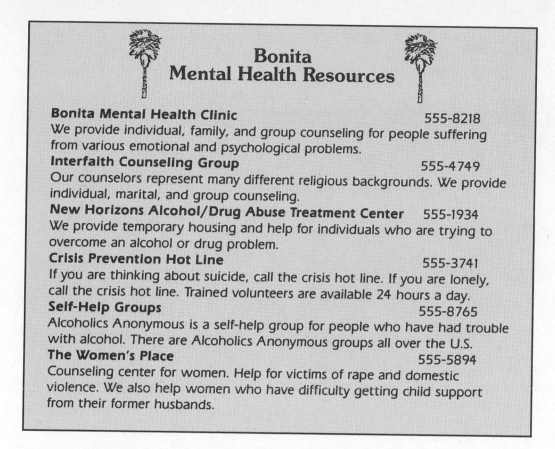

Bonita Mental Health Resources

Bonita Mental Health Clinic   555-8218
We provide individual, family, and group counseling for people suffering from various emotional and psychological problems.

Interfaith Counseling Group   555-4749
Our counselors represent many different religious backgrounds. We provide individual, marital, and group counseling.

New Horizons Alcohol/Drug Abuse Treatment Center   555-1934
We provide temporary housing and help for individuals who are trying to overcome an alcohol or drug problem.

Crisis Prevention Hot Line   555-3741
If you are thinking about suicide, call the crisis hot line. If you are lonely, call the crisis hot line. Trained volunteers are available 24 hours a day.

Self-Help Groups   555-8765
Alcoholics Anonymous is a self-help group for people who have had trouble with alcohol. There are Alcoholics Anonymous groups all over the U.S.

The Women's Place   555-5894
Counseling center for women. Help for victims of rape and domestic violence. We also help women who have difficulty getting child support from their former husbands.

1. Who should you call if a friend has trouble with drugs or alcohol?
2. Who should you call if you are very sad?

In Your Community

Find out the information individually or in groups and share it with the class.

1. What mental health clinics are available in your community? What services do they provide? What do they charge?
2. Are there special clinics for people with substance abuse problems? What services do they provide?
3. What crisis hot lines are there in your community? What services do they provide? What are the telephone numbers? Is there a crisis hot line in your native language?
4. What self-help groups are available in your community?
5. Are there any religious counseling programs in your community?

■ ■ ■ ■ ■ Figuring Out the U.S.

As you read the passage, circle the words you don't understand and try to guess their meanings.

An Advice Column

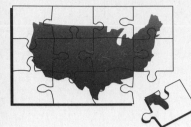

Dear Millie,

I am 43 years old. Up until two years ago, I was a very happy man. I thought nothing could go wrong. Then my wife was killed in an automobile accident. I can't seem to pull myself together. I have tried to be strong for our children. I can't sleep. I have a terrible time eating. I have lost 25 pounds.

I saw my family doctor, and he said I need professional help. He gave me the names of some therapists at the local mental health clinic. I don't know if it will do any good. Please help me. My relatives still live in my native country, so I don't have anyone to talk to. What should I do?

Dan in Denver

Dear Dan,

I think that your doctor gave you a good piece of advice. After a terrible loss such as yours, it is often very difficult to recover. Time doesn't heal all wounds. Sometimes you need the help of a professional. You should find someone you feel comfortable talking with. The job of a therapist is to help you find your own solutions to your problems.

Believe it or not, this letter was written to a stranger. Dan doesn't know Millie. Millie writes an advice column for the newspaper. Thousands of people will read Dan's letter and Millie's answer.

Your Turn

Discuss the questions.

1. Why do you think Dan is asking for advice from a stranger?
2. In your native country, do people talk about their problems, or do they think it is better to keep problems private? Do they talk to strangers? Do they talk to friends or family?
3. If Dan asked you for advice, what would you say? How could different people and agencies help him?

> *Choose one of the questions and write about it.*

Person A

Work with a partner. Look at this page only, and your partner will look at page 60 only.

You are Wei Lei Chu. You need to make an appointment with a doctor at the Bonita Mental Health Clinic. Your partner is Ms. Boulin, the receptionist for Dr. Howard Frankel, a psychiatrist at the clinic. Use your work schedule below to make an appointment.

July	15 Monday	16 Tuesday	17 Wednesday	18 Thursday	19 Friday
7:00			X		X
8:00		X	X		X
9:00		X	X		X
10:00		X	X		X
11:00		X	X		X
12:00	X	X	X		X
1:00	X	X	X		X
2:00	X	X	X	X	X
3:00	X	X		X	X
4:00	X	X		X	
5:00	X			X	
6:00	X			X	
7:00				X	

Person B

Work with a partner. Look at this page only, and your partner will look at page 59 only.

You are Ms. Boulin, the receptionist for Dr. Howard Frankel, a psychiatrist at the Bonita Mental Health Clinic. Your partner is Wei Lei Chu and he or she needs to see Dr. Frankel. Use your appointment book below to schedule an appointment.

July	15 Monday	16 Tuesday	17 Wednesday	18 Thursday	19 Friday
10:00		Ms. Lui	Mr. Romero	Mr. Seltzer	
11:00	Seminar	Ms. Jackson	Ms. Edwards	Ms. Jackson	Ms. Edwards
12:00	Seminar	Lunch	Lunch	Lunch	Lunch
1:00	Seminar	Group Therapy	Group Therapy	Group Therapy	
2:00	Seminar				
3:00					
4:00	Bobby Shepherd	Debbie Jones	Bobby Shepherd		
5:00	Mr. Wester				
6:00		M/M* O'Brien			
7:00		Mr. Pierre	Ms. Charles	M/M Kantor	
8:00		M/M Cohn	Ms. Ruiz	M/M Boetz	

*M/M = Mr. and Mrs.

Before You Listen

1. Who are these people?
2. What do you think they are talking about?
3. What does the man have in his hands?
4. Where did he get it?
5. Where is it from?

■■■■■ Don't You Like Living in the U.S.?

Listen carefully to the dialogue.

Ms. Lin: Hi, Sanjay. How are you?

Dr. Shanmugan: Tired, but fine, thanks. How about you?

Ms. Lin: Fine, thank you.

Dr. Shanmugan: I just got a package from home. My mother sends me packages all the time.

Ms. Lin: That's so thoughtful.

Dr. Shanmugan: She knows living in the United States is hard for me.

Ms. Lin: Don't you like living in the U.S.?

Dr. Shanmugan: No, I don't, Sue. I thought it would be a great place to live.

Ms. Lin: It's not perfect, but the U.S. is much better for me than my native country. We didn't have any freedom there.

Dr. Shanmugan: But I feel like a second-class citizen here. At the hospital they keep on calling me "the foreign doctor." They don't even use my name. If they do, they mispronounce it!

Ms. Lin: Yes. But don't your kids enjoy living in the U.S.?

Dr. Shanmugan: No. They're teased at school because they have accents.

Ms. Lin: But that happens everywhere. I think this is a great place to raise children. In my native country, there were many things that girls couldn't do. Here, my daughters can grow up to be whatever they want to be.

Dr. Shanmugan: Hmm. Yes, that's what my wife says.

Words to Know

freedom	mispronounce	teased
foreign	enjoy	accents

Another Way to Say It

second-class citizen .... a person who is not respected

keep on .... continue

■■■■■ Talking It Over

Discuss the questions in pairs or groups.

1. Why do you think Ms. Lin called Dr. Shanmugan by his first name?
2. Why does Ms. Lin like living in the United States? Look back at the dialogue and find her reasons.
3. Why doesn't Dr. Shanmugan like living in the United States? Look back at the dialogue and find his reasons.
4. What do you like about living in the United States?
5. What could be changed to make living in the United States better?
6. Do people ever mispronounce your name? What do you do or say when they do that?
7. Where do women have more opportunities, in your native country or in the U.S.?

Working Together

Work with your classmates and teacher to finish this conversation. Then practice with a partner.

Mrs. Shanmugan: I like living in the United States. Women are treated as equals here.

Dr. Shanmugan: It's not that bad in our country.

Mrs. Shanmugan:

Dr. Shanmugan:

Real Talk

Yes/no questions often begin with *do* or *does*.

> *Do* you like living in the U.S.?
>
> *Does* your wife like living in the U.S.?

But if you are surprised or don't believe what someone has said, use *don't* or *doesn't*.

> *Don't* you like living in the U.S.?
>
> *Doesn't* your wife like living in the U.S.?

Gerunds and Infinitives

Ms. Lin enjoys	**living**	in the U.S.
She plans	**to live**	in the U.S. forever.

Gerunds	**Infinitives**
Use the *-ing* form	Use the *to* form
after these verbs:	after these verbs:
enjoy (living)	plan (to live)
like*	need
avoid	want
finish	hope
keep on	expect
The gerund refers to a	The infinitive refers to a
present or past activity.	future activity.

Like can also take the *to* form.

Practice A

Complete each sentence with the correct form of a verb from this list.

be	**call**	**pronounce**
feel	**live**	**study**

1. Mrs. Shanmugan enjoys _*living*_ in the U.S.

2. Her daughters plan _____ medicine.

3. They want _____ doctors.

4. Dr. Shanmugan doesn't like _____ in the U.S.

5. People keep on _____ him "the foreign doctor."

6. He expects people _____ his name correctly.

7. He doesn't want _____ like a second-class citizen.

Practice B

Work with a partner. Ask and answer questions about things you want to do in the future and things you enjoy doing.

Example: *Do you want to go to a movie tomorrow?*
Do you enjoy going to the movies?

■■■■■ Read and Think

Read the passage and try to guess the meanings of the underlined words. Rephrase each paragraph.

Communications

In the United States, people use the telephone and mail to <u>communicate</u> with one another.

Telephone companies in the U.S. are privately owned. They are not owned by the government. There are two types of telephone <u>companies</u> in the U.S. Local telephone companies provide <u>service</u> for the community.

There are also many <u>long-distance telephone carriers</u>. These companies give you service so that you can make telephone calls outside your city and in different states and countries. Usually, there are several long-distance telephone companies to choose from. You must decide which long-distance carrier you want to use.

Some have better <u>rates</u> for <u>international</u> telephone calls, but others have other advantages. You should describe the kinds of calls that you usually make each month so that each long-distance carrier can tell you what it offers. Then you need to make the decision.

Another way of communicating is through the U.S. Postal Service. You can send letters and packages through the U.S. mail. Different prices are charged for sending letters and packages. The price depends on where your mail is going, how fast you want it to get there, and how heavy it is. There are competitors for package delivery and <u>overnight delivery</u>. However, the U.S. Postal Service is the only <u>inexpensive</u> delivery service for letters.

In Your Community

Work in small groups. Find out the least expensive long-distance telephone rates for places you often call.

1. Make a list of distant places that you and your classmates call frequently. Include places that are within and outside the U.S.
2. Have each member of your group contact one long-distance company. Ask for the lowest charge for a three-minute call and the least costly time to call. Make a chart like the following one.

Long-Distance Carrier	Place Called	Cheapest Time to Call	Price of 3-Minute Call

As you read the passage, circle the words you don't understand, and try to guess their meanings.

The Morning Mail

Mohammed has just received a lot of mail. He is very tired and doesn't know what he should read first. Look at the following mail. Decide which mail is junk mail and which is personal mail that needs his attention. Junk mail is mail used to sell or advertise a product.

Your Turn

Discuss the questions.

1. What kind of mail do you get?
2. What types of junk mail do you get?
3. Do you write or receive many personal letters here?
4. Do you like getting letters? Do you like writing letters?
5. Have you ever had trouble getting mail from your native country? If you have, what did you do?

> *Choose one of the questions and write about it.*

11 | Should I Call the Police?

Before You Listen

1. Who are these people?
2. Where are they?
3. Why do you think Maureen is calling Mrs. Cogam (Ruth Cogam's grandmother)?

■ ■ ■ ■ ■ Should I Call the Police?

Listen carefully to the dialogue.

Mrs. Cogam: Hello.

Maureen: Hi, Mrs. Cogam. This is Maureen O'Brien. I'm babysitting Billy Tamler. I didn't know if I should call you . . . Anyway, I'm calling because there's something strange going on here . . .

Mrs. Cogam: You did the right thing, Maureen. I'm the leader for the neighborhood crime watch program. What's happening?

Maureen: Well, I put Billy to bed, and then the cat started acting upset. I looked out the window, and I saw a van out front. There were two men in it. Then I started hearing funny noises like someone was crawling around on the roof.

Mrs. Cogam: Have you called Mr. and Mrs. Tamler?

Maureen: Yes, but they're at the baseball game. I called the baseball stadium, and they get people only in case of an emergency. I don't know if this is an emergency. Should I call the police?

Mrs. Cogam: Is the van still there?

Maureen: That's the strange thing. The van is still out front. But now there is only one man in it. Oh no! I just heard the doorbell. Should I call the police? What should I do?

Words to Know

babysitting   stadium   _____

crime watch   _____   _____

Another Way to Say It

going on .... happening

out front .... outside in front of (the building)

funny .... odd

_____ .... _____

■ ■ ■ ■ ■ Talking It Over

Discuss the questions in pairs or groups.

1. Why do you think Maureen called Mrs. Cogam?
2. Do you think Maureen is scared? Do you think she should be scared?
3. What should Maureen do?
4. Who do you think is at the front door?
5. Should Maureen call the police?
6. In your native country, who takes care of the children when their parents go out?
7. How old do you think someone should be to babysit?
8. In your native country, do you open your door to strangers? Why or why not?

Working Together

Work with your classmates and teacher to finish this conversation. Then practice with a partner.

911 Operator: Hello, emergency operator.
    Maureen: Hello, please send someone to help me!
911 Operator: What's the problem, Miss?
    Maureen:
911 Operator:

Real Talk

Anyway is used in conversation to get back to the point of a conversation or to end the conversation.

    Anyway, I'm calling because there's something strange going on here.
    Anyway, I'll talk to you later.

Embedded Questions

Yes/no questions can be embedded in a sentence. The question is changed to a clause beginning with *if* or *whether*. They have the same meaning here.

Should I call you?

I didn't know **if** I should call you.

I didn't know **whether** I should call you.

Use sentence word order when you make an embedded question.

Practice A

Mr. and Mrs. Tamler decided to make their house more secure. There are some questions they cannot answer. Give their answers using either *I don't know* or *I'm not sure*. Use the first one as an example.

1. Should we put another lock on the door?

I don't Know if we should put a new lock on.

2. Do we have a neighborhood watch committee on this block?

_____

3. Can we get windows that can't be broken?

_____

4. Has this house ever been broken into?

_____

5. Will the police check our house every day while we are on vacation?

_____

Practice B

Write sentences about the security of your home. You are not sure if you should make these changes.

Example: *I don't know if we should get a watch dog.*

■■■■■ Read and Think

Read the news about neighborhood crime. Rephrase each paragraph. Then answer the questions.

Bonita Daily News

Crime Beat

The following crimes were reported in the past 24 hours. These are crimes that have not been solved. If you have any information about these crimes, please contact the Police Department at 555-8764.

Purse Snatching

Three purse snatchings were reported in Nathaniel Park. The suspect is a white male in his mid-twenties. He has blond hair and green eyes. He robs older women walking with canes.

Burglary

A house on Cypress Street and Washington Avenue was burglarized yesterday during the day. A television set, computer, and microwave oven were stolen.

Arson

A fire started in an old building near Redwood High School. A gasoline can was set on fire. Three people were hurt.

Car Theft

A yellow sports car was stolen from the Value Way supermarket parking lot. The license plate number is 876 BET.

Rape

A young white female jogger was raped at gunpoint in the Groveland Park area at about six in the morning. The victim described the attacker as about 18 years old with a scar on his upper right cheek. He also had very short black hair and brown eyes.

---

1. Which crime has a suspect?
2. Which crime has a description of the criminal?
3. Which crime do you think is the worst? Why?
4. Do crimes like these happen in your native country?
5. What do people in your native country do to prevent or stop crime?

In Your Community

Form groups according to your community.

Make a list of crimes that have recently occurred in your area. Work as a group to find ways to prevent these crimes from happening again.

■■■■■ Figuring Out the U.S.

As you read Ms. Jones's speech, circle the words you don't understand and try to guess their meanings.

Under the Influence

Many of you know me as Rebecca Jones. I used to be the president of the Bonita Savings Bank. I was a well-liked and respected member of the community. I had a lovely home, lovely children, and a loving husband. I was a very happy woman. That was the story of my life until five years ago.

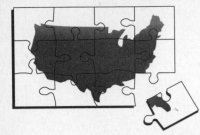

Five years ago, we had a Christmas party at the bank for bank employees. I drank a lot of rum punch. When it was time to go home, several of my employees said that they would drive me because I was too drunk to drive. I told them that I was fine and that I could handle it.

It was dark that night, and I didn't see a man who was crossing the street. I was also going too fast. I hit and killed the man crossing the street. He had three children and a wife. I felt like I was a real criminal, a murderer. I had never done anything to hurt anyone before.

I spent two years in jail for manslaughter. I never thought of myself as a bad person until that night. I know that there are three children who will grow up without a father. There is a woman who became a widow because of me. I have a hard time living with myself.

My husband divorced me. My children visited me in jail. I was fired from the bank. I will never have a job as good as the one I had at the bank, all because of drinking.

Your Turn

Discuss the questions.

1. What was Rebecca Jones's job? Why did she lose her job?
2. Do you think it was right for her to lose her job?
3. Why do you think she gave the speech?
4. What laws against drunk driving does your state have? Check with your local Motor Vehicles Facility. Do you think that these laws are too weak?
5. What laws against drunk driving does your native country have?

> *Choose one of the questions and write about it.*

Before You Listen

1. Do you remember these people?
2. Where are they?
3. What do you think Global Care is?
4. What do you think *beautification* means?

▪▪▪▪▪ Think Globally, Act Locally

Listen carefully to the dialogue.

Mrs. Park: Thank you for coming. We want to tell you about the Global Care beautification project.

Mr. O'Brien: What is Global Care?

Mrs. Tamler: Global Care is a non-profit organization. As you know, Bonita Soups finally went under last year. Global Care bought the factory and has just opened up a recycling plant.

Dr. Shanmugan: What do they recycle?

Mr. Samuels: We make old bottles, cans, and newspapers into new products. I work at Global Care with Mrs. Park and Mrs. Tamler.

Mrs. Tamler: Bonita will be a better place to live.

Dr. Shanmugan: I hope so.

Mr. Samuels: Global Care is offering our community up to $2,000 for projects that will make Bonita a better place to live.

Mrs. Park: Their motto is "Think globally, act locally." They'll give money for projects that will make Bonita look nicer.

Mrs. Cogam: The neighborhood crime watch needs new radios and flashlights.

Mrs. Tamler: Well, I think they have beauty in mind more than safety.

Mrs. Samuels: What about new benches at the bus stops?

Mr. O'Brien: How about a community garden?

Words to Know

global	recycling plant	locally
beautification	products	project
non-profit	motto	benches

Another Way to Say It

went under .... went out of business

recycle .... make ready for reuse

up to .... not more than

_____ .... _____

■ ■ ■ ■ ■ Talking It Over

Discuss the questions in pairs or groups.

1. What is Global Care?
2. Why does Mr. Samuels say "we"?
3. Why do you think Global Care wants to give money to the community?
4. What projects will Global Care not give money for?
5. What does the motto "Think globally, act locally" mean?
6. Do you think a private company should pay for public projects like this?
7. Do you think recycling is important? Why or why not?
8. How do people in your native country feel about recycling?

Working Together

Work with your classmates and teacher to finish this conversation. Then practice with a partner.

Ruth Cogam just finished a can of soda and is throwing it into the trash.

Grandmother Cogam: Don't throw away that can, Ruth.
   Ruth Cogam: What should I do with it?
Grandmother Cogam:
   Ruth Cogam:

Real Talk

What about and *How about* are very common sentence starters for suggesting something. Note that they are not complete sentences, but they are very common in informal spoken English.

  What about new benches at the bus stops?
  How about a community garden?

What about is often pronounced "Whaddabout."
How about is often pronounced "How 'bout."

Expressing Opinions

You can express opinions with the following verbs:

I **think** [that] . . .   I **don't think** [that] . . .

He **believes** [that] . . .   He **doesn't believe** [that] . . .

She **agrees** [with] . . .   She **disagrees** [with] . . .

Mr. O'Brien **thinks** they should have a community garden.

Mrs. Tamler **agrees with** him.

Practice A

Use the information in the chart to complete the sentences below. Choose from the opinion verbs above.

	Mr. O'Brien	Mrs. Samuels	Mrs. Cogam
wants	community garden new benches	new benches safety equipment	safety equipment community garden
doesn't want	safety equipment	community garden	new benches

1. Mr. O'Brien _thinks they should start a community garden._

2. Mrs. Samuels _____ Mr. O'Brien about the garden.

3. Mrs. Cogam _____ they should buy safety equipment.

4. Mr. O'Brien _____ her.

5. Mrs. Samuels _____ new benches.

6. Mr. O'Brien _____ with Mrs. Samuels.

7. Mrs. Cogam _____ Mr. O'Brien about the garden.

Practice B

Recycling is good for the environment, but it is difficult and takes a lot of time. Take an opinion poll in your class and write the results using *think*, *believe*, and *agree (with)* or *disagree (with)*.

Example: *Kyoko thinks recycling is important.*
Ahmed disagrees with her.

Read the passage and try to guess the meanings of the underlined words.
Rephrase each paragraph.

Conserving Our Natural Resources

The United States is such a large country that people used to think its
<u>resources</u> were <u>unlimited</u>. However, Americans are discovering that there are
limited supplies of water, electricity, and <u>fuel</u>. In many parts of the country,
there are already water <u>shortages</u>. People in the U.S. need to <u>conserve</u> water,
electricity, and fuel, or we will <u>run out</u> in the future.

You can also save money when you use less water, electricity, and fuel.
Many apartments and houses are charged for the amount of water,
electricity, or fuel they use. The less you use, the less you pay.

Here are some tips for saving these important resources:

Saving Water

Never leave water running. Take quick showers. Showers use less water than
baths. Use a sponge and a bucket to wash cars instead of a garden hose.

Saving Electricity

Turn lights off when you leave a room if you're going to be gone for more
than 10 minutes. Buy <u>energy-saving</u> light bulbs. Don't use a washer or dryer
unless it is full.

Saving Fuel

People use fuel to heat homes, to cook, and to make cars run. Save heating
fuel by keeping your house or apartment at 68 <u>degrees</u> in the winter. Try to
use your oven during the coldest part of the day, and it will heat up the
kitchen as it cooks the food. Drive your car more slowly. If you have to wait
for someone, turn off your engine.

In Your Community

Find out the information in small groups and share it with the class.

1. Call your local water or electricity company, and find out more ways you
   can save water and energy. Ask for pamphlets or for someone to come to
   your home and teach you how to save.
2. Ask your classmates how they save water and energy. Make a group list of
   ways to conserve water and energy.

■ ■ ■ ■ ■ Figuring Out the U.S.

As you read the passage, circle the words you don't understand and try to guess their meanings.

It's Getting Better!

I remember when I first moved to this neighborhood five years ago. It was the only place that I could afford. There were lots of drug dealers near my apartment building. I wouldn't let my children go outside, because I was so afraid. The neighborhood was dirty, and no one seemed to care about

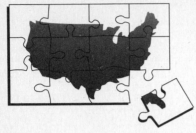 anything. Things are better now. The community worked together to get rid of the drug dealers. Now it is a safer place to live.

I remember just three years ago how awful this building looked. There was lots of graffiti all over the building. Kids had written nasty things on most of the building. I live on the 10th floor, and the elevator was broken all the time. I was very ashamed to tell people where I lived. Things are better now. The neighborhood got together and started to clean up the place. We painted the buildings. We planted some trees and built a playground for our children. People have begun to care. It's getting better.

Your Turn

Discuss the questions.

1. What can you do to make your community look better?
2. Is your neighborhood safe? Why or why not?
3. What can you do to make your neighborhood free from drugs?
4. How can you make your neighborhood a good place for children and senior citizens?
5. Do people in your native country work together to make their neighborhoods safe?

> *Choose one of the questions and write about it.*

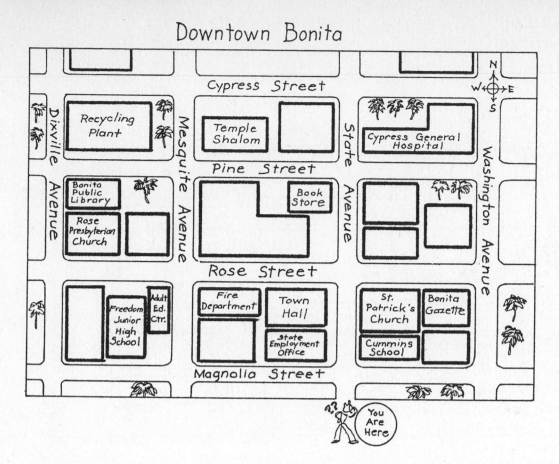

Downtown Bonita

Person A

You need directions to the **American Legion Hall,** the **Medical Office Building, Bay View Apartments, Roma Nova Restaurant,** the **Bonita Police Department,** and **Redwood High School.** Your map shows these buildings but does not show their names. Your partner's map does show the names. Ask your partner for directions to these places. Be sure to tell your partner where you are right now. Use words. Do not point. Do not look at each other's maps until you are finished.

Later, your partner will ask you for directions to places that are named on your map.

When you finish, there will still be some buildings with no names. Work together to decide what these places are. (Two buildings do not have names on either map. Decide with your partner what they should be.) Write the names on the buildings. Draw another person somewhere on your map, and write directions to get your person to the buildings you just labeled.

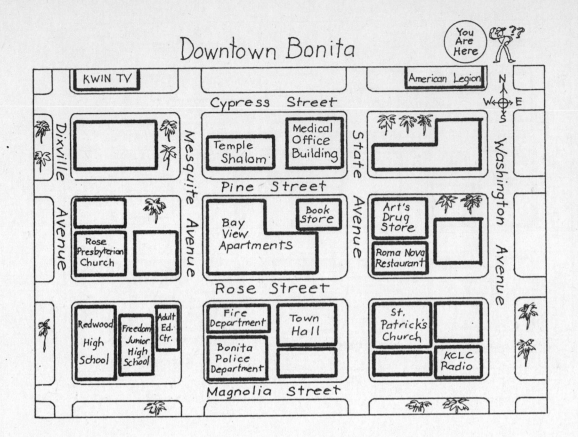

Downtown Bonita

Person B

You need directions to the **recycling plant, Cypress General Hospital, Bonita Public Library,** the **State Employment Office, Cummins School,** and the *Bonita Gazette*. Your map shows these buildings but does not show their names. Your partner's map does show the names. Ask your partner for directions to these places. Be sure to tell your partner where you are right now. Use words. Do not point. Do not look at each other's maps until you are finished.

Your partner will ask you for directions to places that are named on your map.

When you finish, there will still be some buildings with no names. Work together to decide what these places are. (Two buildings do not have names on either map. Decide with your partner what they should be.) Write the names on the buildings. Draw another person somewhere on your map, and write directions to get your person to the buildings you just labeled.

Appendix

■■■■■ Community Resources for *Discovering Your Community*

Complete the chart below with information about your community. Most of these organizations are listed in your telephone directory.

Community Name _____

Your Name _____

Chapter Topic	Organizations/ Resources	Local Organization Name	Telephone Number in Your Community
1 Entering a new community	Adult education center		
	Community college		
	Private/Specialty Schools		
2 Unemployment	Employment office		
	Social Security Office		
	Public Aid Office		
	State Tax Office		
	Internal Revenue Service		
3 Community organizations	Churches		
	Ethnic organizations		
	Neighborhood groups		
	Business/civic groups		
4 Emergency communications	Radio news		
	Television News		
	Local newspapers		
5 Information and entertainment	Cable television stations		
	Bilingual radio/TV stations		
	Movie theater		
	Newsletters		
6 Library	Local library		
	Reference librarian		
	Children's librarian		

Chapter Topic	Organizations/ Resources	Local Organization Name	Telephone Number In Your Community
7 Recreation and fitness	Recreation center		
	Health club		
	Local sports leagues		
8 Public transportation	Bus (local)		
	Bus lines (long-distance)		
	Rapid transit		
	Trains (long-distance)		
9 Mental health	Mental health clinic		
	Crisis hot line		
	Battered women's shelter		
	Alcoholics Anonymous (AA)		
	Al-Anon		
	Churches, religious organizations		
10 Communication (mail/telephone)	Post Office		
	Local telephone company		
	Long-distance service		
11 Crime prevention	Police Department		
	Crime Watch		
	Victim assistance counseling		
	Rape crisis center		
12 Community improvement	Community representative		
	Neighborhood organizations		
	Recycling centers		

Cut this out and keep it next to your telephone.

■ ■ ■ ■ ■ Irregular Verbs in *Discovering Your Community*

Basic Form	Simple Past	Past Participle
be	was/were	been
beat	beat	beaten
become	became	become
begin	began	begun
break	broke	broken
bring	brought	brought
broadcast	broadcast	broadcast
buy	bought	bought
choose	chose	chosen
come	came	come
cost	cost	cost
do	did	done
drink	drank	drunk
drive	drove	driven
eat	ate	eaten
feed	fed	fed
feel	felt	felt
find	found	found
fit	fit	fit
fly	flew	flown
forget	forgot	forgotten
get	got	gotten (or got)
give	gave	given
go	went	gone
grow	grew	grown
have	had	had
hear	heard	heard
hold	held	held
hurt	hurt	hurt
keep	kept	kept
know	knew	known
lay	laid	laid
leave	left	left
let	let	let
lose	lost	lost
make	made	made

Irregular Verbs in *Discovering Your Community* (cont.)

Basic Form	Simple Past	Past Participle
mean	meant	meant
meet	met	met
overcome	overcame	overcome
pay	paid	paid
put	put	put
quit	quit	quit
read	read	read
ride	rode	ridden
run	ran	run
say	said	said
see	saw	seen
send	sent	sent
speak	spoke	spoken
spend	spent	spent
stand	stood	stood
swim	swam	swum
take	took	taken
tell	told	told
think	thought	thought
understand	understood	understood
withhold	withheld	withheld
write	wrote	written

■■■■■ Index

*These words and phrases are found in the **Words to Know** and **Another Way to Say It** sections.*